P9-DGW-809

BY THOMAS K. ADAMSON

THE INDIANAPOLIS
COLTS
STORY

TORQUE
™

BELLWETHER MEDIA · MINNEAPOLIS, MN

Are you ready to take it to the extreme? Torque books thrust you into the action-packed world of sports, vehicles, mystery, and adventure. These books may include dirt, smoke, fire, and chilling tales. **WARNING**: read at your own risk.

This edition first published in 2017 by Bellwether Media, Inc.

No part of this publication may be reproduced in whole or in part without written permission of the publisher. For information regarding permission, write to Bellwether Media, Inc., Attention: Permissions Department, 5357 Penn Avenue South, Minneapolis, MN 55419.

Library of Congress Cataloging-in-Publication Data

Names: Adamson, Thomas K., 1970-
Title: The Indianapolis Colts Story / by Thomas K. Adamson.
Description: Minneapolis, MN : Bellwether Media, Inc., 2017. | Series:
    Torque: NFL Teams | Includes bibliographical references and index. |
    Audience: Ages: 7-12. | Audience: Grades: 3 through 7.
Identifiers: LCCN 2016005866 | ISBN 9781626173682 (hardcover : alk. paper)
Subjects: LCSH: Indianapolis Colts (Football team)–History–Juvenile
    literature.
Classification: LCC GV956.I53 A35 2017 | DDC 796.332/640977252–dc23
LC record available at http://lccn.loc.gov/2016005866

Printed in the United States of America, North Mankato, MN.

TABLE OF CONTENTS

The Indianapolis Colts face the New York Jets on January 24, 2010. It is the American Football **Conference** (AFC) Championship game. The Jets build a lead in the first half. Colts' **quarterback** Peyton Manning stays calm.

Peyton Manning

4

Austin Collie

He throws an 18-yard pass to **wide receiver**
Austin Collie. The next play is a 46-yard pass to
Collie. Finally, Manning finds Collie in the end
zone. Touchdown!

Pierre Garçon

The Colts are still behind at halftime, but not for long. In the third quarter, Manning throws a perfect pass. Wide receiver Pierre Garçon makes an amazing catch in the end zone. The Colts take the lead!

Indianapolis never looks back. They win 30 to 17. On to **Super Bowl** 44!

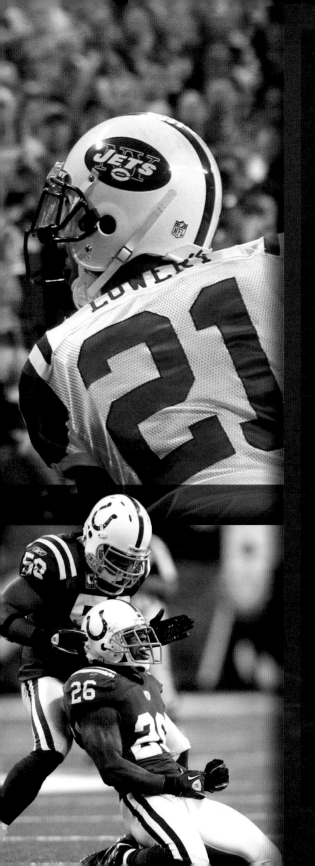

SCORING TERMS

END ZONE
the area at each end of a football field; a team scores by entering the opponent's end zone with the football.

EXTRA POINT
a score that occurs when a kicker kicks the ball between the opponent's goal posts after a touchdown is scored; 1 point.

FIELD GOAL
a score that occurs when a kicker kicks the ball between the opponent's goal posts; 3 points.

SAFETY
a score that occurs when a player on offense is tackled behind his own goal line; 2 points for defense.

TOUCHDOWN
a score that occurs when a team crosses into its opponent's end zone with the football; 6 points.

TWO-POINT CONVERSION
a score that occurs when a team crosses into its opponent's end zone with the football after scoring a touchdown; 2 points.

The Colts are a tough team to beat in the National Football League (NFL). They missed the **playoffs** only three times from 2000 to 2015.

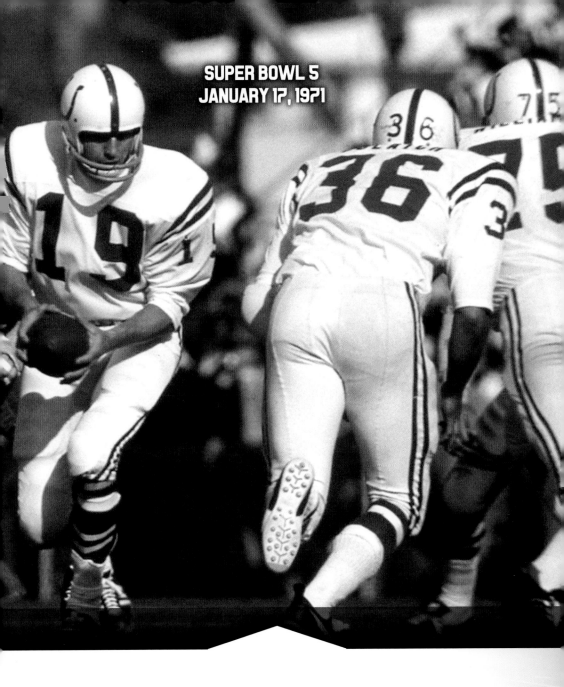

They are from Indianapolis, Indiana, but used to play in Baltimore, Maryland. The Colts have won championships in both cities!

Lucas Oil Stadium is a sea of blue on game days. This home of the Colts and their fans is in downtown Indianapolis.

Its **retractable** roof can open or close in about 9 minutes. It is the largest retractable roof in the NFL!

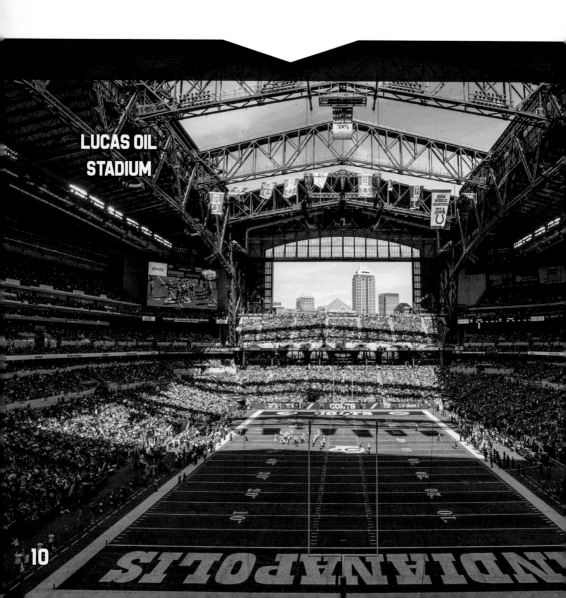

LUCAS OIL STADIUM

INDIANAPOLIS,
INDIANA

N
W━━E
S

The Colts play in the South **Division** of the AFC. For years, the Colts' path to the Super Bowl seemed blocked by their main AFC **rival**. The New England Patriots were hard to beat.

In 2007, the Colts defeated the Patriots in the AFC Championship. They went on to win Super Bowl 41!

NFL DIVISIONS

AFC

AFC NORTH

BALTIMORE **RAVENS**

CINCINNATI **BENGALS**

CLEVELAND **BROWNS**

PITTSBURGH **STEELERS**

AFC EAST

BUFFALO **BILLS**

MIAMI **DOLPHINS**

NEW ENGLAND **PATRIOTS**

NEW YORK **JETS**

AFC SOUTH

HOUSTON **TEXANS**

INDIANAPOLIS **COLTS**

JACKSONVILLE **JAGUARS**

TENNESSEE **TITANS**

AFC WEST

DENVER **BRONCOS**

KANSAS CITY **CHIEFS**

OAKLAND **RAIDERS**

SAN DIEGO **CHARGERS**

NFC

NFC **NORTH**

CHICAGO
BEARS

DETROIT
LIONS

GREEN BAY
PACKERS

MINNESOTA
VIKINGS

NFC **EAST**

DALLAS
COWBOYS

NEW YORK
GIANTS

PHILADELPHIA
EAGLES

WASHINGTON
REDSKINS

NFC **SOUTH**

ATLANTA
FALCONS

CAROLINA
PANTHERS

NEW ORLEANS
SAINTS

TAMPA BAY
BUCCANEERS

NFC **WEST**

ARIZONA
CARDINALS

LOS ANGELES
RAMS

SAN FRANCISCO
49ERS

SEATTLE
SEAHAWKS

13

In 1953, the NFL's Dallas Texans moved to Baltimore. The team was renamed the Baltimore Colts. By 1958, the team became known for winning often.

Legendary quarterback Johnny Unitas was a big part of their success. In less than 15 years, the Colts were NFL champions three times.

GREATEST GAME EVER PLAYED

People still talk about the 1958 NFL Championship game. They call it the "Greatest Game Ever Played." The Colts beat the New York Giants 23 to 17 in overtime!

Johnny Unitas

After 1971, the team had many losing seasons. The Colts' owner moved the team to Indianapolis in 1984.

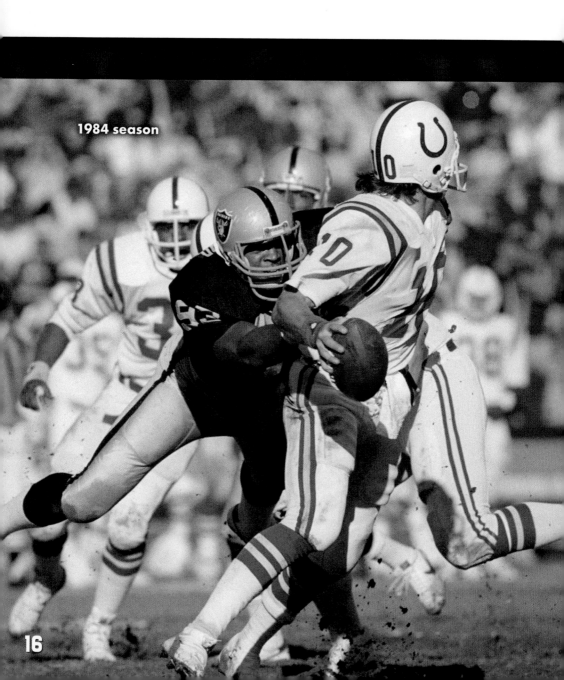

1984 season

MOST VALUABLE QUARTERBACK

Manning was named Most Valuable Player (MVP) five times in his career. Four of those times were with the Colts.

It took a while for the Indianapolis Colts to build a winning team. In 1998, they **drafted** Peyton Manning. That choice brought many years of success.

COLTS TIMELINE

1953

Won first regular season game, beating the Chicago Bears

13 FINAL SCORE **9**

1971

Won Super Bowl 5, beating the Dallas Cowboys

16 FINAL SCORE **13**

1959

Won second straight NFL Championship, beating the New York Giants (31-16)

1968

Played in Super Bowl 3, but lost to the New York Jets (7-16)

1956

Signed Hall-of-Fame quarterback Johnny Unitas

1984

Moved to Indianapolis and became the Indianapolis Colts

2008

First played in Lucas Oil Stadium

1998

Drafted quarterback Peyton Manning

2010

Played in Super Bowl 44, but lost to the New Orleans Saints

17   FINAL SCORE   **31**

2007

Won Super Bowl 41, beating the Chicago Bears

29   FINAL SCORE   **17**

2012

Drafted quarterback Andrew Luck

Many football fans say Johnny Unitas was the best quarterback ever. He was a great leader and calm in difficult moments. Later, Peyton Manning became a star on the field.

Peyton Manning

Johnny Unitas

Jeff Saturday

Marvin Harrison

COUNT UP THE CATCHES!

In 158 games, Manning and Harrison teamed up for 953 completions. Together, they made 112 touchdowns!

Center Jeff Saturday was Manning's main protector on **offense**. Wide receiver Marvin Harrison caught hundreds of Manning's passes. He had a great ability to get open.

On **defense**, Gino Marchetti was quick and tough. Opposing quarterbacks did not like to play against him. Dwight Freeney had incredible speed for a **defensive lineman**. He made over 100 **sacks** during his career with the Colts.

Today, quarterback Andrew Luck is a strong leader for the Colts. On top of that, he is a great sport.

TEAM GREATS

GINO MARCHETTI
DEFENSIVE END
1953-1964, 1966

JOHNNY UNITAS
QUARTERBACK
1956-1972

MARVIN HARRISON
WIDE RECEIVER
1996-2008

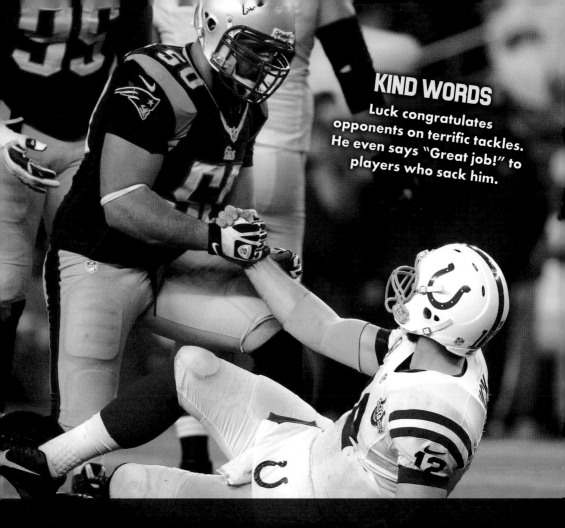

Luck congratulates opponents on terrific tackles. He even says "Great job!" to players who sack him.

PEYTON MANNING
QUARTERBACK
1998-2010

JEFF SATURDAY
CENTER
1999-2011

DWIGHT FREENEY
DEFENSIVE END
2002-2012

Fans in Indiana have supported the Colts since they first moved to the state. The team has kept many old traditions. The horseshoe logo on the helmet has been the same since 1957.

The team colors have stayed the same for more than 60 years. Fans like the classic style of blue and white.

Many Colts fans **tailgate**. A good number are in a fan club called the Blue Crew.

These fans have their own parking lot where they gather to eat and get excited for the game. They go crazy for their team. It is even more intense when the Patriots are in town!

MORE ABOUT THE
COLTS

Team name:
Indianapolis Colts

Team name explained:
Named after Baltimore's
history of horse racing;
the team kept "Colts"
when it moved to
Indianapolis in 1984.

Joined NFL: 1953

Conference: AFC

Division: South

**Main rivals: New England
Patriots, Houston Texans**

Hometown:
Indianapolis, Indiana

Training camp location:
Anderson University, Anderson, Indiana

INDIANA

INDIANAPOLIS

N
W — E
S

Home stadium name:
Lucas Oil Stadium

Stadium opened: 2008

Seats in stadium: 67,000

Logo: A blue horseshoe

Colors: Blue and white

Name for fan base: Blue Crew

Mascot: Blue

GLOSSARY

center–a player on offense whose main jobs are to pass the ball to the quarterback at the start of each play and to block for the quarterback

conference–a large grouping of sports teams that often play one another

defense–the group of players who try to stop the opposing team from scoring

defensive lineman–a player on defense whose main job is to try to stop the quarterback; defensive linemen crouch down in front of the ball.

division–a small grouping of sports teams that often play one another; usually there are several divisions of teams in a conference.

drafted–chose a college athlete to play for a professional team

legendary–famous for being good at something

offense–the group of players who try to move down the field and score

playoffs–the games played after the regular NFL season is over; playoff games determine which teams play in the Super Bowl.

quarterback–a player on offense whose main job is to throw and hand off the ball

retractable–able to open and close

rival–a long-standing opponent

sacks–plays during which a player on defense tackles the opposing quarterback for a loss of yards

Super Bowl–the championship game for the NFL

tailgate–to have a cookout in the parking lot at a sporting event; a tailgate is also the door at the back of a pickup truck that flips down.

wide receiver–a player on offense whose main job is to catch passes from the quarterback

TO LEARN MORE

AT THE LIBRARY

Gilbert, Sara. *The Story of the Indianapolis Colts*. Mankato, Minn.: Creative Education, 2014.

Scheff, Matt. *Superstars of the Indianapolis Colts*. Mankato, Minn.: Amicus, 2014.

Zappa, Marcia. *Indianapolis Colts*. Minneapolis, Minn.: ABDO Publishing, 2015.

ON THE WEB

Learning more about the Indianapolis Colts is as easy as 1, 2, 3.

1. Go to www.factsurfer.com.

2. Enter "Indianapolis Colts" into the search box.

3. Click the "Surf" button and you will see a list of related web sites.

With factsurfer.com, finding more information is just a click away.

INDEX